Please return

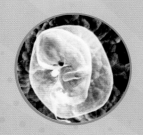

GROWING UP

Humans From Birth To Old Age

Jen Green

raintree 🍃

a Capstone company — publishers for children

Raintree is an imprint of Capstone Global Library Limited, a company incorporated in England and Wales having its registered office at 264 Banbury Road, Oxford, OX2 7DY – Registered company number: 6695582

www.raintree.co.uk
myorders@raintree.co.uk

Edited by Helen Cox Cannons
Designed by Cynthia Della-Rovere
Original illustrations © Capstone Global Library Limited 2018
Picture research by Kelly Garvin
Production by Kathy McColley
Originated by Capstone Global Library Limited
Printed and bound in India

ISBN 978 1 4747 6626 5
22 21 20 19 18
10 9 8 7 6 5 4 3 2 1

British Library Cataloguing in Publication Data
A full catalogue record for this book is available from the British Library.

Acknowledgements
We would like to thank Dr Jonathan Cardwell FRCPCH, Consultant Paediatrician with the Northumbria Healthcare NHS Foundation Trust, for his invaluable help in the preparation of this book.

We would like to thank the following for permission to reproduce photographs: Dreamstime/Connie Larsen, 20, 22; iStockphoto: FatCamera, 21 (bottom), gradyreese, 18, Ranta Images, cover; Shutterstock: 2p2play, 1 (top right), 28 (bottom left), Aila Images, 29 (middle left), alexassault, cover, Alinute Silzeviciute, 16 (top), Angela Luchianius, 15 (top), Anna Kraynova, 15 (bottom), Blend Images, 17 (bottom), BlueRingMedia, 7, 21 (top), 23 Boris Medvedev, 14 (bottom), Bosnian, 16 (bottom), Cheryl E. Davis, 13 (bottom), Christian Darkin, 1 (top left), 28 (top left), Dragon Images, 25 (bottom), Flashon Studio, 28 (middle left), Gelpi, cover, Giovanni Cancemi, 6, Iaremenko Sergii, 9 (bottom), Jiri Hera, 1, (top middle), 28 (middle right), Josep Curto, 1 (bottom right), 29 (bottom right), jstudio, 29 (top left), lanych, 17 (top), Luis Louro, 1 (bottom left), 28, (bottom right), Monkey Business Images, 4, 8, 24, 27, mrvirgin, 12 (right), Oksana Kuzmina, 13 (top), pablofdezr, 10-11, Paul Hakimata Photography, 1 (bottom middle), 29 (top right), pixelheadphoto digitalskillet, 25 (top), Purino, 14 (top), Rawpixel.com, 1 (bottom middle), 29 (bottom left), rnl, 29 (middle right), Roman Samborskyi, cover, Rose Carson, 12 (left), Rostislav Stach, 5, Sergey Nivens, 8-9 (background), sylv1rob1, 9 (top), travelview, 19, u3d, 28 (top right), Vecton, 11, wavebreakmedia, 26; SuperStock/CHASSENET/BSIP, cover. Artistic elements: Shutterstock: 3RUS, Amicabel, Curly Pat.

CONTENTS

Some words in this book appear in bold, **like this**. You can find out what they mean by looking in the glossary.

INTRODUCTION

What is your earliest memory? Can you remember learning to walk, talk or read? You are part-way through the journey of life. It began before you are born and will continue into old age. This book plots the stages in that journey.

How are we different?

Humans are **mammals**, like cats, dogs, monkeys and horses. Our big brains set us apart from other animals. Our intelligence allows us to understand many things, including how life begins, why children look like their parents and how we grow to become adults.

Humans take a long time to grow up. It will be many years before this toddler can look after herself.

Reproduction

The **life cycle** of all living things includes **reproduction**. Like many animals and plants, humans reproduce sexually. Males and females come together to produce young. Birds and reptiles reproduce sexually by laying eggs. In mammals, including humans, babies develop inside the mother. After birth, mammal babies feed on milk.

A young fox learns to hunt by copying its mother.

Mammals growing up

Most mammals grow up much more quickly than humans. A young mouse leaves the nest after just 18 days. By 6 to 9 months old, a dog is able to **mate** and have puppies. Mammals such as elephants and chimpanzees stay with their mother for several years, learning the skills they need to survive as adults. Humans take the longest time of all to grow up, perhaps because we have so much to learn.

Chapter 1:
LIFE BEGINS

Your body is made of billions of tiny units called **cells**. It can be hard to believe that you began when just two cells **combined** to become one.

Fertilization

In **sexual reproduction**, life begins when a male cell and a female sex cell unite. You began when a tadpole-like **sperm** from your father's **testes** joined with an **ovum**, or egg cell, from your mother's **ovaries**. This happens during sex, when sperm released by the man's **penis** swim up through the mother's **womb** into tubes that lead to the ovaries. There, one sperm joins with a ripe egg, and **fertilization** takes place.

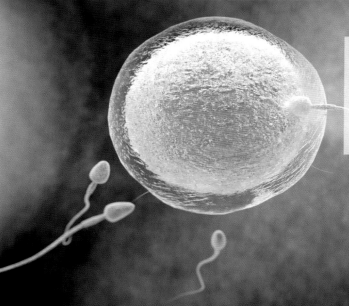

A tiny sperm fuses with the larger ovum. The fertilized egg will develop into a baby.

The fertilized egg divides to become two cells, then four, eight and so on. By Day 5, a ball of about 100 cells has formed. It drifts down into the womb, and sinks into the blood-rich lining, which supplies it with nourishment. The developing baby is called an **embryo**.

The developing embryo

As cell division continues, the baby's head and backbone form, then the arms and legs. By eight weeks, the embryo has fingers, toes and a face. It's still tiny – about the size of a kidney bean.

Twins

If two eggs from the ovaries are fertilized by two sperm, non-identical twins develop. These can be different sexes. If one fertilized egg splits into two halves that both develop, identical twins are the result. The identical twins are either both boys or both girls.

4 weeks

10 weeks

16 weeks

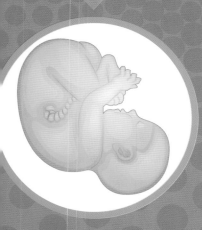

20 weeks

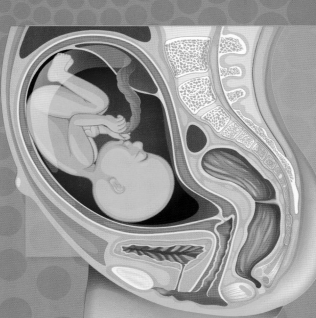

At around 8 weeks old, the embryo becomes a **foetus**. The foetus gradually looks more human as features such as face and limbs form. For more on the development of the foetus, see chapter 2.

Genes and inheritance

Have you ever been told you look like your mum or dad? People may say you have your father's eyes, or your mother's hair. Children resemble (look like) their parents because the fertilized egg cell from which you developed contained coded instructions, called **genes**, from both parents. Genes tell cells how to grow, work and develop. They control inherited features such as eye, hair and skin colour.

Children resemble their parents because of genes.

Chromosomes

Genes are found on x-shaped structures called **chromosomes**. These are inside the **nucleus** of cells. Humans have 46 chromosomes. Almost every cell in your body contains a full set of chromosomes, but sex cells have only a half-set. When the egg and sperm fuse, the two half-sets combine to make a full set of instructions – the code for a **unique** person.

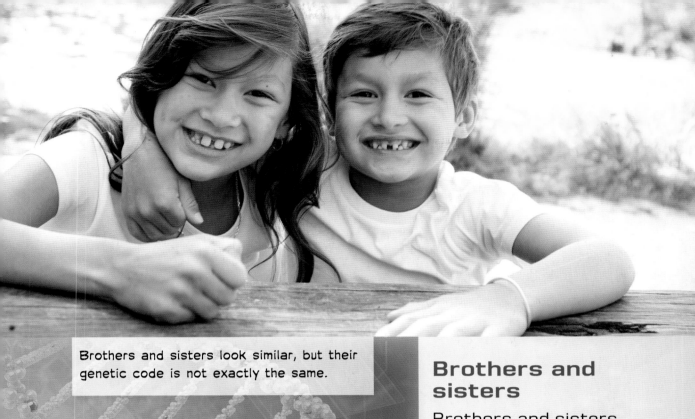

Brothers and sisters look similar, but their genetic code is not exactly the same.

Brothers and sisters

Brothers and sisters often resemble each other, but aren't exactly alike because each sperm and egg cell contains a slightly different mix of genes. This creates a unique combination of genes every time. Only identical twins have exactly the same genes.

Boy or girl?

The **gender** (sex) of babies is decided by two chromosomes, called the x and y chromosomes. The mother's chromosome is always x, the code for a girl. The father's chromosome may be either x or y. Y is the code for a boy. If the father adds an x, the child will be a girl. If he adds a y, it will be a boy.

Chapter 2:
UNBORN BABY

By 10 weeks old, the baby's main body parts have developed, but it is still tiny. The unborn child, now called a foetus, spends most of its time sleeping, but may also yawn, hiccup, cough and stretch. At around 20 weeks, many mothers start to feel their baby kick.

Nourishment

The unborn foetus doesn't breathe through its nose or eat with its mouth. Instead it is nourished (fed) by an organ called the **placenta**. A tube called the **umbilical cord** connects the foetus to the placenta, where its blood flows alongside the mother's. **Nutrients** and oxygen from the mother's blood pass to the foetus, and waste passes out.

Birth

At 40 weeks, the fully developed baby is ready to be born. The protective sac breaks, and the fluid flows out. The walls of the womb squeeze, gently at first, then more strongly, to push the baby out. Most babies are born head-first.

GROWTH OF A FOETUS

At 28 weeks the foetus is about half its birth weight. At 38 weeks it reaches full size.

embryo
8 weeks

foetus
12 weeks

16 weeks

20 weeks

24 weeks

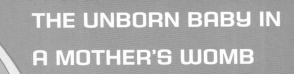

THE UNBORN BABY IN A MOTHER'S WOMB

Placenta provides nourishment and oxygen

Wall of womb

Umbilical cord leads from the baby's belly button to the placenta

Amniotic sac is a fluid-filled bag which protects the baby from knocks

Neck of womb

This well-developed baby is almost ready to be born.

Gestation

The time the baby spends in the womb is called **gestation**. Small mammals such as mice and rabbits take only 3–4 weeks to develop. Human babies take 40 weeks (9 months). Only female whales and elephants are pregnant for longer – whales for 10–15 months and elephants for 22 months.

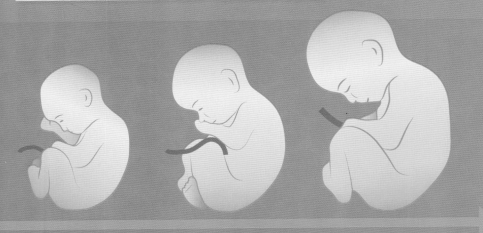

| 28 weeks | 31 weeks | 36 weeks | 40 weeks |

Chapter 3:
BABY

Moments after being born, a baby takes its first breath. Most babies cry as they sense the bright and noisy world around them. A doctor or nurse cuts the umbilical cord that connected the mother with her unborn baby.

First weeks

Newborn babies are very helpless. Mammals such as lambs and foals can stand just a few minutes after birth. In contrast, a human baby can't even sit without help or hold its head up. The baby is mostly asleep, but cries if it feels hungry, tired, cold or uncomfortable.

Baby reflexes

Newborn babies have natural reflexes that help them survive the first months of life. A baby will naturally grasp anything put into its hands, and cries to get attention. Sucking is a natural reflex that allows the baby to drink its mother's milk.

Movement and coordination

A newborn baby has no control over its movements. However, as it kicks and waves its arms, its muscles grow stronger, and gradually it learns how to use them. By six months old a baby can roll over, lift its head and grasp objects. By eight months it is able to sit without help, and by nine months it is crawling on hands and knees. At about one year old, a child stands and takes its first steps. By now it can handle small objects.

Growth

Babies grow fastest in the womb and in the first year of life. A newborn baby measures around 51 centimetres long and weighs an average of 3.5 kilograms. By its first birthday, a baby has grown by about 25 centimetres and has tripled its birth weight.

Chapter 4:
TODDLER

About two months after taking its first steps, a child starts to toddle. Between the ages of one and three an infant learns a huge amount – how to **coordinate** movements and also how to talk.

Movement

Physical skills increase greatly between the ages of one and three. Between the ages of one and two, toddlers' walking improves and they learn to run. They also learn to throw and kick, and push and pull objects along. They learn how to fit objects together.

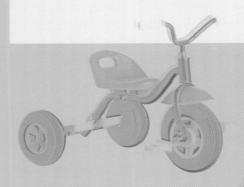

All in our genes?

Genes alone do not control how we grow and develop. Experience and upbringing also play a part. For example, you inherit a general body type from your parents, but diet and exercise will affect how you grow, and your height and weight.

Talking

Young babies coo and babble as they copy sounds made by their parents. At around one year old, they start to say their first real words. Between the ages of one and two, babies learn to link words together to make simple phrases. Gradually they form more complicated sentences.

Social skills

Learning to talk allows a child's social skills to develop. Parents encourage children to share toys and consider the feelings of others. The child learns to feed itself and use the potty. He or she is becoming more independent.

Chapter 5:

CHILD

Starting school is a huge milestone in life. Can you remember your first day at school? Everything seemed so strange at first, but soon became familiar.

At school

The primary school years are a time of almost constant learning. Children learn to read and write. They begin to study subjects such as Maths and Science.

Riding a bike involves skill and coordination, as you balance on the wheels, steer with your hands and pedal with your feet.

Body proportions

Body proportions change throughout childhood. Babies have a very large head, short body and rounded limbs. As we grow older the body and limbs grow faster than the head. Adults have a relatively small head in proportion to their body size.

Playing sport and doing gym increase your strength and make you more **supple**.

New skills

Between the ages of three and nine, confidence grows as children learn new skills and become more independent. Children gain new physical skills, such as learning to swim, riding a bike and turning a cartwheel. At the same time, they master technology such as smartphones and computers. Social skills increase as children learn to make decisions and plan for the future. Children's ideas and opinions continue to develop into adulthood.

Growth

Infants grow faster than older children. After the age of two, growth slows but continues steadily. A child's height increases at an average of 6 centimetres each year. As the body grows and limbs get longer, children begin to take on an adult shape.

17

Chapter 6

PUBERTY

Between the ages of 9 and 14 or 15, our bodies change quite fast as we grow up to become adult. These physical changes are called **puberty**. We also grow up mentally as we prepare for adult life. This time is called **adolescence**.

Puberty can be an emotional roller-coaster, as moods change fast.

Physical changes

During puberty both girls and boys quickly get taller. Body shape changes, and hair starts to grow around the **genitals** and other places. We also sweat more, so hygiene becomes important. A girl's **periods** start.

These changes are due to body chemicals called **hormones**. These are made in the **pituitary gland** in the brain and in the reproductive organs – the girl's ovaries and the boy's testes (testicles).

Timing

Puberty happens at slightly different times in girls and boys. Girls generally pass puberty between the ages of eight and fourteen. In boys, puberty happens a little later, between the ages of nine and fifteen. But timing also varies between individuals.

Mood changes

Puberty is a time of emotional upheaval. Many young people experience mood swings. You may feel happy and excited one moment, then sad or angry the next. You may feel self-conscious about physical changes that are happening to you. You may feel strongly attracted to others. All of this is quite normal, so try not to worry about it.

Acne

During puberty the skin becomes more oily. Oil and dead skin can block openings in the skin called **pores**, causing spots or **acne**. Don't squeeze spots. A healthy diet may help acne to go away, and it will probably clear up after puberty. If acne doesn't clear up, a doctor may be able to help.

Puberty in girls

At puberty, a girl's ovaries start to produce the female hormone **oestrogen**. This triggers changes to the reproductive organs and other body parts.

Puberty brings changes to a girl's body.

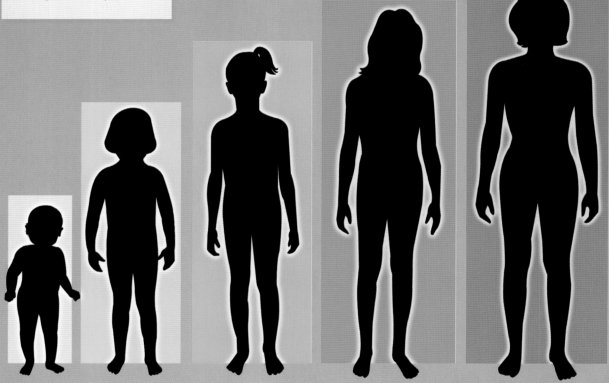

Physical changes

A girl's breasts start to swell, and she may find it more comfortable to wear a bra. The hips get wider. Hair grows under the armpits and around the genitals. The ovaries start to release a ripe egg every month, and monthly bleeding starts. These changes make it possible for a girl to have a baby.

THE FEMALE REPRODUCTIVE ORGANS

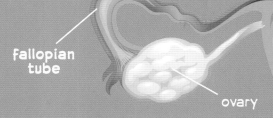

womb

fallopian tube

ovary

ovary

fallopian tube

neck of womb

Periods

Monthly bleeding is called **menstruation**. At puberty the **menstrual cycle** begins. Once every 28 days, the lining of the womb thickens to prepare for a baby to grow if an egg is fertilized. If this doesn't happen, the lining breaks down and passes out of the **vagina** as a small flow of blood. The bleeding lasts for a few days and varies from month to month and person to person. **Sanitary towels** and **tampons** soak up the trickle of blood.

Coping with periods

Before a period, some girls and women feel irritable or have headaches. This is called **premenstrual tension (PMT)**. During your period, you may feel a dull ache in your stomach. If this is slight, exercise can ease it. If it's more painful it can help you to rest with a hot water bottle on your tummy. You can be as active as you like during your period, including playing sport.

21

Puberty in boys

Puberty usually happens a little later in boys, between the ages of ten and fifteen. The testes start to produce the male hormone **testosterone**, which triggers changes throughout the body.

During puberty, changes happen to turn a boy into a man.

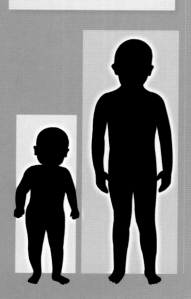

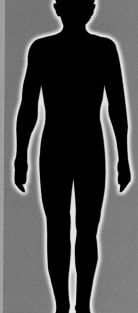
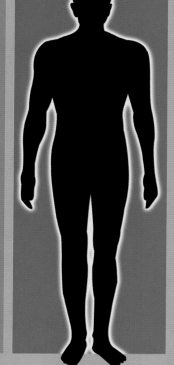

Physical changes

The growth spurt in boys comes a little later than girls, after the age of ten. Hair begins to grow under the armpits, around the genitals and also on the face, chest and sometimes other places. The chest and shoulders broaden and the body becomes more muscular.

The testes get larger inside the skin pouch called the **scrotum**. The penis gets larger too. The testes start to produce millions of sperm a day. These are stored in a coiled tube called the **epididymis**, unless they exit through the penis, in a milky fluid called **semen**.

THE MALE REPRODUCTIVE ORGANS

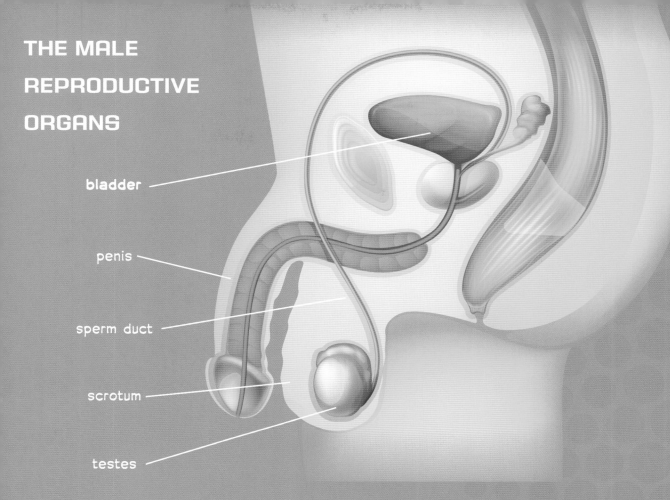

bladder

penis

sperm duct

scrotum

testes

Sexual feelings

Like girls, boys develop strong feelings for others. Sexual feelings can cause an **erection**. This is when the penis becomes stiff and hard. Sperm may discharge from the penis – this is called **ejaculation**. If this happens at night, simply mop it up with a tissue. All of this is perfectly normal and part of growing up, as your reproductive system starts to work.

Breaking voice

At puberty the boy's voice box gets larger, causing a lump called the Adam's apple to form in the throat. The voice becomes deeper quite suddenly. You may sound gruff one moment and squeaky the next, as you learn to control your new voice.

Chapter 7:

ADULT

After puberty, you possess an adult body! You are now physically able to be a mother or a father. Most people find that it's better to wait until your twenties or thirties to start a family.

Sex

In your late teens or as a young adult, you may have your first relationship – another major step in life. If you meet someone and fall in love, you may choose to have sex. Love-making or **sexual intercourse** starts with kissing and cuddling. The man's penis

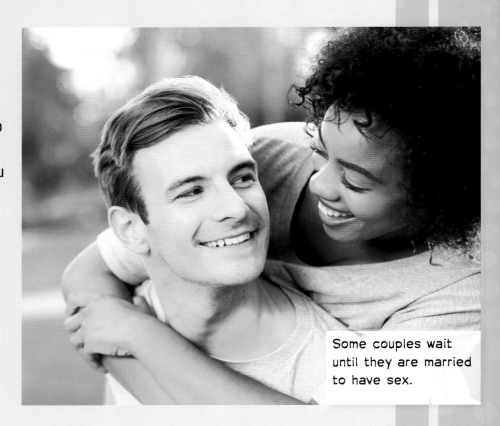

Some couples wait until they are married to have sex.

rises and stiffens so it fits into the woman's vagina. At the climax of love-making, semen squirts from the penis. Sperm swim up through the womb. If a sperm unites with an egg, a new human life begins.

Making choices

Having a baby is a huge decision. Many couples use **contraception** to prevent fertilization until the time is right. There are many forms of contraception. You may also choose not to have sex with a partner. No one should feel pressured into having sex if they don't want to. Part of being an adult is making your own decisions about your life.

Contraception can help couples choose when to start a family.

Staying healthy

In early adulthood, school or college ends and working life begins. Throughout life it's important to get the right balance between work, rest and play. Doctors recommend taking regular exercise to stay fit and keep at a healthy weight. Eating a balanced diet and getting enough sleep will also help you stay healthy.

Chapter 8

GROWING OLDER

In your twenties, you reach your full height and peak fitness. But men's muscles continue to develop. The body carries on changing throughout life. But these changes happen much more gradually, so they are hardly noticeable for many years.

Growing families

Between the ages of 20 and 40, many couples start a family. As the years pass, their children grow up and may have children of their own. One day you could become a grandparent, though it's hard to imagine that right now!

Many people continue to be fit and active until late in life.

Ageing

As time passes, the body ages. As skin ages it becomes less elastic and wrinkles form. (Sunshine also ages skin.) Hair turns grey, and men's hair gets thinner. Around the age of 50, a woman's ovaries stop producing eggs and her periods stop. This is called the **menopause**. Men carry on being **fertile** for longer.

Retirement

In their sixties, most people stop work – another major life change. As the years pass, the senses begin to weaken and the body becomes less flexible. People may get ill as body parts wear out. However, with regular exercise and a good diet, many people stay fit and healthy well into retirement.

Lifespans

Humans live considerably longer than most animals. Mice live three to four years. Dogs live for 10-15 years. Blue whales can live for 35 years and elephants for 70 years. A century ago, few people lived much beyond 60. Now, thanks to modern medicine, many people live on into their seventies, eighties or even nineties.

Many families include three or even four **generations** as people live longer.

TIMELINE

Follow the flow chart to trace the journey of a human life.

EMBRYO: 0–8 WEEKS

Human life begins as a sperm fertilizes an egg. The tiny baby, called an embryo, develops in its mother's womb.

FOETUS: 8 WEEKS– 9 MONTHS

The baby, now called a foetus, continues to grow and develop.

BABY: 0–1 YEARS

Helpless at first, the baby learns to support its head, sit up, crawl, stand and take its first steps. It learns to use its senses and gains control over its limbs.

BIRTH

After 40 weeks in the womb the baby is born.

TODDER: 1–3 YEARS

Walking improves, then running. The child learns to push and pull objects along, fit things together and feed itself. He or she learns to talk.

YOUNG CHILD: 3–6 YEARS

The child learns toilet training. Talking and physical skills continue to improve. As school begins, the child learns to read and write.

OLDER CHILD: 6-10 YEARS

The child is learning new ideas and skills. He or she continues to grow about 5 centimetres each year.

PUBESCENT: 10-14 YEARS

The child grows quickly as puberty begins. A girl's breasts swell and her periods start. A boy's testes start producing sperm and his voice "breaks".

YOUNG ADULT: 18-35 YEARS

The body reaches its full height, strength and fitness. Many couples start a family as well as going to work.

OLDER TEENAGER: 14-18 YEARS

During the late teens, the body continues to become more adult. Boys become more muscular. School ends and college or working life begins.

MIDDLE-AGED ADULT: 35-55 YEARS

The body ages and skin starts to wrinkle, but adults are still as active as they wish. Between the ages of 45 and 55 women go through the menopause.

OLDER ADULT: 55+ YEARS

Working life ends and retirement begins. The body continues to age and become less flexible, but the adult gains wisdom and experience.

GLOSSARY

acne skin condition involving spots, which often affects teenagers around puberty

adolescence period, which begins with puberty, when a child develops into an adult

amniotic sac fluid-filled bag in which the baby develops in the womb

bladder sac where urine is stored before you wee

cell one of the tiny units of which living things are made

chromosome x-shaped structure found inside cells, which contains genes

combine come together

contraception device or technique to prevent a girl or woman becoming pregnant

coordinate when different parts, such as parts of the body, work together effectively

ejaculation when semen comes out of the penis

embryo unborn baby that is less than eight weeks old

epididymis coiled organ where sperm are stored

erection when the penis becomes stiff

fallopian tube egg tube leading from the ovary to the womb

fertile able to have children

fertilization moment when the sperm joins with an egg, and a new life begins

foetus unborn baby developing in the womb, between 8 and 40 weeks old

gender whether an animal is male or female

gene chemicals inside cells that pass on inherited features, such as eye or hair colour

generation all the people born about the same time

genital body part involved in reproduction

gestation period between fertilization and birth, during which a mother is pregnant

hormone substance made by the body that affects a certain body function

life cycle all the stages an animal passes through in its lifetime, as it is born, grows and becomes adult and eventually dies

mammal type of animal whose young drink their mother's milk. Dogs, cats, apes and humans are mammals.

mate when a male and female come together to produce young

menopause when a female stops producing eggs and monthly bleeding ends

menstrual cycle monthly cycle of females, which includes producing ripe eggs and menstruation (bleeding)

menstruation monthly flow of blood in women and girls, also called a "period"

nucleus control centre of a cell

nutrient substance that provides nourishment

oestrogen female sex hormone that becomes active during puberty

ovary female organ that produces ova (eggs)

ovum (plural ova) female sex cell or egg

penis male organ used to transfer sperm and also urinate (pee)

period *see* menstruation

pituitary gland gland in the brain which affects growth and development. A gland is an organ that releases a body chemical.

placenta blood-rich organ in the womb that nourishes the unborn baby

pore tiny opening in the skin

premenstrual tension (PMT) symptoms that affect some girls and women before their periods start

puberty stage in the human life cycle when the reproductive organs start working and a child starts to become adult

reproduction *see* sexual reproduction

sanitary towel disposable pad worn to soak up blood lost during menstruation

scrotum bag of skin that contains the male testes

semen whitish liquid that contains sperm

sexual intercourse sexual act that involves a man's penis entering a woman's vagina

sexual reproduction when a male and female mate and produce young

sperm male sex cell made by the testes

supple bendy, flexible

tampon cotton plug inserted into the vagina to absorb blood during menstruation

testis (plural testes) male testicle, the organ that produces sperm

testosterone male sex hormone that becomes active during puberty

umbilical cord cord that joins the unborn baby to the placenta

unique unlike anything else

vagina tube that leads from the womb to the female genitals

womb organ inside a woman's body where a baby develops

FIND OUT MORE

Books

Inheritance and Reproduction, Jen Green (Raintree, 2014)

Puberty and Growing Up, Anna Claybourne (Franklin Watts, 2016)

The Boy's Guide to Growing Up, Phil Wilkinson (Wayland, 2016)

The Girl's Guide to Growing Up, Anita Naik (Wayland, 2016)

What's Happening to Me? (Girl), Susan Meredith (Usborne, 2015)

What's Happening to Me? (Boy), Alex Frith (Usborne, 2015)

Website

KidsHealth offers information and advice about puberty:

kidshealth.org/en/kids/puberty.html

Childline offers advice and support for children:

www.childline.org.uk

Find out more about the human life cycle on this website:

www.dkfindout.com/uk/human-body/life-cycle

INDEX